The Gift of
Small
Potatoes

How a Culture of Generosity
Empowers Mission-Driven Brands
to Win Trust, Earn Loyalty, and
Unlock Abundance

BRIAN G. SOOY

First edition

ISBN: 9798585718373

This book was professionally typeset on Reedsy.
Find out more at reedsy.com

For my wife, Lisa.

We're more generous together.

Contents

III   Part Three

Preface

I have a close friend who loves to do good for others.

When she hears of a need, she'll spend hours searching for the best way to meet the need so she can bless people.

Once, when she heard a family desperately needed new home appliances, she blessed them by having them delivered anonymously.

As a parent, she feels the pain of mothers whose daughters are trafficked and enslaved.

As a woman of faith, she feels compassion for the poor, the hurting, and the persecuted.

She's a financial wizard when it comes to managing money and making an impact.

She's hesitant to support collective impact, community investment funds, or other vehicles where she perceives her gifts' impact is diluted.

Is she philanthropic? Of course, she is!

Does she conform to the philanthropy sector's definition of philanthropy?

It depends on who you ask. You might call her an everyday philanthropist, but she simply thinks of herself as generous.

She's not wealthy by some people's standards, but over a lifetime her gifts add up.[1]

If you were to ask her why she gives, she says, "I love to be generous, and it brings me joy," and that's what matters.

* * *

Before you read further, here's my disclaimer: This book is not written by a fundraising executive, professional researcher, or nonprofit executive.

That being said, nonprofits with which I've consulted have generated millions in revenue by changing the way they approach fundraising by focusing on the value of relationships over the function of philanthropy.

I write with the perspective of a donor, former board member, and friend to generous people.

As a design professional with decades of practical and data-driven experience, I'm writing it to give you a different perspective — outside of your frame of reference — that I believe will either spark a conversation or make you wish you didn't buy this book.

Designers tend to see the world as it is and as it could be, and as such, we solve problems (we call that practice design thinking) to meet the need of the person who experiences the problem, not the need of the person trying to solve the problem. When you define a problem the right way, you can end up solving your problem as well.

It's an ethnographic approach where we put ourselves in the audience's place and understand the world through their eyes and experience.

When an organization's brand is rooted in the four dimensions of culture — purpose, character, communications, and voice — its leader can weave a culture of generosity throughout the fabric of people, perceptions, and practice with which generous people interact.

Culture is based on your organization's values, revealed in its character, and demonstrated in its actions.

Think of your brand's values as the deeply held beliefs that form your organization's character and guides its actions. When brand personality and behavior align and work in harmony, people create a perception of your organizational culture that nurtures trust, authenticity, and credibility.

Whether it's time, talent, or treasure, we all invest in that in which we believe. Everyone has the capacity for generosity,

While that may seem obvious, the practice of nurturing relationships with people who care deeply about their values and the causes that inspire them is often secondary to the functional aspect of fundraising.

If you've become jaded about fundraising and tired of chasing donors, this book is for you.

I'm writing to remind you to think of the people you ask for money as generous people who want to participate in a generous culture.

Real philanthropy helps people align their assets and generosity with what they say is important to *them*.

When you inspire people with a grateful heart to view fundraising as stewardship and not a management function, they are more likely to succeed with their goals.

When you inspire people because you begin the relationship with a grateful and generous heart, you're more likely to succeed in your goals.

I want you to experience the joy of helping people give and find deeper fulfillment in your philanthropy work.

Acknowledgement

Thanks to the contributors who shared their insights back in 2016 and 2017: Morgan Roth, Lauren Steiner, Megan Constantino, Brian Frederick, Cecilia Render, Deborah Hoover, Laura Malone, and Tom Ahern.

Although it took me four years to complete this work, thank you for being generous with your thoughts, insights, and time!

I

Part One

*"When I think of philanthropy, I think of billionaires
and millionaires.
Everybody can be generous."*

—*The Everyday Giver*

1

Is Philanthropy a Practice or a Virtue?

Organizations such as the Evelyn & Walter Haas Jr. Fund commissioned research and white papers to define and standardize what "culture of philanthropy" means for the nonprofit and philanthropic sector. It's excellent research that focuses on standardization, processes, and systems with recommendations for organizations to improve their cultural practices.

Cynthia M. Gibson's paper, "Beyond Fundraising: What Does it Mean to Build a Culture of Philanthropy,"[2] and Simone Joyaux's essay, "Building a Culture of Philanthropy in Your Organization,"[3] are resources worth exploring.

Flipping the Philanthropy Conversation on its Head

Let's look at this from another perspective: Building a philanthropy culture focuses on equipping the *practitioner* instead of inspiring and engaging the *donor*. A fundraiser can't go to a supporter and tell them they must practice a culture of philanthropy. The supporter won't understand the inside language used to describe a fundraiser's cultural practice.

Simone Joyaux expresses this problem in her white paper, *Building a Culture of Philanthropy in your Organization,*

> *"A culture of philanthropy refers to your organization's attitude toward philanthropy and fund development (fundraising)."*
>
> *"Why is a culture of philanthropy so important? Because philanthropy is not just about raising money. Philanthropy (and fundraising) is not just another management function."*
>
> *Simone Joyaux*

Generosity is a Virtue, not a Management Function

Cultural practice and behaviors are based on core values (character), whether they are stated or defined. Culture is how you do things in your organization or business. Values define a brand's character; culture is character and values in action.

If you were to ask a person on the street, they might tell you that philanthropy focuses on two key aspects: asking people for money and giving away money.

Most people have been approached by one or more charities asking for donations and, in this context, see themselves as donors. These same people would consider Bill and Melinda Gates (if they are aware of them at all) or high-profile donors within their communities as "philanthropists."

Support isn't limited to financial contributions. I can be an ambassador or advocate for a cause without donating a dime. The problem is that many organizations view people as donors, instead of donors as people.

That's why we're using the word *supporter, giver,* or *gift-giver* for this book because a supporter gives of their time, talent, and treasure.

Instead of looking inward, let's look at creating a culture of philanthropy with our focus on the gift-giver:

> *"A culture of generosity refers to your organization's attitude toward its supporters, their charitable goals, and the impact they hope to achieve.*
>
> *Why is a culture of generosity so important? Because generosity is not just about raising money, it's about inspiring and enlightening people to give from their abundance. Stewardship is not just another management function; it's a relational dynamic that empowers donors to become who they want to be so they can experience the joy of giving."*
>
> Brian Sooy

The virtue of generosity is not merely an approach to fund development or supporter-focused communications; it's a core value—a fundamental belief that guides how you and your organization integrate the *practice* of philanthropy into your work and mission every day.

> *Generosity frames how you integrate philanthropy (the practice of being generous) into your brand and culture.*

When we focus on generosity as a core value of an organization's culture, we begin with a simple premise:

> *Generous people possess an abundance of resources and*

the desire to share those resources in ways that allow them to make a difference for a cause in which they believe or about which they care.

It's not my goal to repeat the findings and framework from other research (although I will reference it). I want to look at it from the supporter's perspective.

I invite you to explore perspectives from practitioners, consultants, and professionals whose work influences and impacts generosity and culture in the organizations in which they work.

But first, a story...

2

The Gift of Small Potatoes

An everyday giver, my friend showed me a thank you card she received after making a financial gift to a charity.

"Even though it's signed," she began, "it's a form letter. I would expect a more personal response to a gift of this size, even if it's from staff or a board member. To me, this says my donation is no more important than a $50 gift."

She lamented, "I know my gift is not as large as others they receive; I'm just small potatoes. But my "small potatoes" could have a significant impact on a smaller organization. This was a sacrifice for me."

$1,000 or $2,500 may seem like small potatoes to your organization.

A $2,500 gift could have a significant impact when given to a small nonprofit. In this case, it would be a minor gift when contributed to a capital or major gifts campaign.

Instead of thinking of a financial donation as a gift, what if you considered it as a sacrifice that an individual made to support your cause and advance your mission?

She concluded, "I don't expect recognition; that's not why I give. But I don't like how this acknowledgment made me feel."

* * *

How will you acknowledge the smaller financial gifts that your donors entrust to your care?

How you acknowledge a supporter's financial sacrifice will leave an impression that will last for years. *Consider what the gift means to the giver.* Call and ask why the gift was made — you'll understand your donor more meaningfully and nurture the relationship in a profound way.

An individual may forget what you do or say in response to their gift, but they won't forget how you made them feel.

Would you rather have a supporter share why they are disappointed with how their gift was acknowledged or how thoughtful it was when you called them?

The giver makes a financial donation that by all appearances is transactional. You accept the donation, check the acknowledgment box, and get one step closer to your goal.

The supporter is really giving you their *trust* and goodwill and sharing their desire for generosity. They are placing a part of themselves into your hands as a way of standing for your cause and deepening their relationship with you.

If she thinks your cause is worthy, a supporter is more likely to donate. In the case of the everyday giver, she may decide to give elsewhere. She is the one who decides what cause is worthy of her gift.

The true exchange a customer makes when they make a gift to your cause is trust. Money is simple proof of the exchange.

The everyday philanthropist, the generous giver, may not want recognition.

They want authentic recognition that their gifts and generosity are meaningful and that your organization is grateful for the ~~gift~~ sacrifice they made, no matter what size.

How you respond to an act of generosity is an outward indicator of your brands' internal culture of generosity.

When you respond in a way that leaves a lasting impression, you can harvest more than potatoes. How you acknowledge a supporter's gift may be the last time you can win their trust and earn their loyalty.

3

Generosity is a Branding Challenge

According to the CAF World Giving Index[4], the United States scores over 50% in being generous, revealing an untapped opportunity to develop a culture and a mindstate of generosity, particularly among those who don't view themselves as generous.

When we think of a person as generous, we're describing a character virtue. If philanthropy is a practice and generosity is a virtue, why is the philanthropic and nonprofit sector so focused on practice and technique instead of brand character, organizational culture, and donor motivations that unlock the experience of that virtue?

The question of whether your organization embraces a culture of generosity as branding, or more accurately, a brand identity issue is worth considering.

Do supporters identify your organization as nurturing and facilitating generosity, where their desire for generosity/desire to be charitable can be realized through opportunities to do something right, make a difference, and become who they want to be?

Fostering a culture of any kind is a branding process: What supporters and people think about your brand's purpose, character and culture create perception. To the supporter, perception is reality.

How people perceive your organization cannot be controlled, but how you contribute to culture and influence their perception can be intentional.

What will it take for your organization to be perceived as one that practices and nurtures generosity, advocates for supporter's interests, and welcomes generosity?

If your organization relies on donations or external funding, leaders will ask:

- What are our supporter's aspirations and goals?
- How can we help them achieve their aspirations and goals?
- How can we help fulfill their goals and become more generous?

Next, you must ask: Why do people give, or why are people generous?

- To support a cause
- To create change or specific impact.
- To fulfill a personal need.
- In response to personal experience
- To express legacy through shared values.

Generosity is a Mindstate

When I modeled the idea of donor motivations that align with the National Taxonomy of Exempt Organizations[5] in, *Raise Your Voice: A Cause Manifesto*[6], I explored the idea from experience and intuition. I did not include a research-based understanding of emotional, mindstate marketing. I stated:

> *"After researching donor and volunteer motivations, some patterns emerges with regard to reasons (motivations) and values. Some causes appeal to the heart more than they speak to the mind. Others speak to the mind — to inform before they inspire — and appeal to personal factors.*
>
> *Ask some of your current donors and volunteers why they do what they do on behalf of your cause. The answers will give you great insight into how you can communicate more effectively with them."*
>
> From "You Are Here: The Cause Quadrant," *Raise Your Voice: a Cause Manifesto*, page 39

Then I discovered the science that backs up my intuition.

William Leach, behavioral researcher and author of *Marketing to Mindstates: The Practical Guide to Applying Behavior Design to Research and Marketing*[7], suggests we consider the emotional factors that make people more susceptible to influence. By understanding and activating the temporary, nonconscious mindstates that heavily influence consumers' decisions, we can understand what motivates them to be generous and then message those motivations.

These principles can help you create a culture of generosity.

When you ask why a person wants to be generous, you begin to understand five key factors:

1. Their functional goals (*what* they want to accomplish),
2. The giver's high-order goals (*why* they want to give),
3. Their motivations (Success, independence, connection, mastery, control, fulfillment, respect, appreciation, safety),[8]
4. Their approach to giving (To promote or prevent something they care about),
5. The triggers that influence their decision-making.

Not only are supporters looking for organizations whose values and goals align with their own, but they also want to be part of a community of people who give to causes they share a mutual affinity for.

Why? Supporters want to achieve specific goals that align with whom they aspire to be.

A culture of generosity does not accept the status quo: it recognizes there may be a better way and is open to making it a reality. The problem is we're uncomfortable with new. We're uncomfortable with new processes, new approaches. We're uncomfortable with measuring the results we achieve, for fear they do not measure up to the board's (and our supporter's) expectations.

"Design is the silent ambassador of your brand," stated the legendary designer Paul Rand. For the mission-driven organization, design thinking connects strategy, message, and mission with your staff, prospects, donors, advocates, boards, and influencers.

For the philanthropic leader, your rallying cry can be, "Design is the silent ambassador of our cause."

A high-performing, mission-driven organization needs to be innovative and disruptive in how it pursues design thinking with purpose and clarity of communication to create a culture of generosity. It must seek ways to change supporters' expectations, surprise its funders, and illuminate its work outcomes to new audiences.

4

What Defines a Culture of Generosity?

Specifically, the Evelyn & Walter Haas Jr. Fund report, "Underdeveloped: A National Study of Challenges Facing Nonprofit Fundraising," frames the concept of a culture of philanthropy in the context of an organization with a culture that supports fundraising success:

> *"Most people in the organization (across positions) act as ambassadors and engage in relationship-building. Everyone promotes philanthropy and can articulate a case for giving. Fund development is viewed and valued as a mission-aligned program of the organization. Organizational systems are established to support donors. The executive director is committed and personally involved in fundraising."*

For our purposes, we redefine a culture of philanthropy as a *culture of generosity*, shifting us from an inward focus on organizational practice to an external focus on the wants and desire of the supporter:

"An organization models and practices a culture of gen-erosity when an individual's values and desire for gen-erosity align with opportunities for impact that transform the supporter, steward trust, and build affinity for the cause."

Generous Culture Follows the Individual

When the focus on a culture of philanthropy is specific to an organization, it opens a gap where people split their thinking between work and charity.

Fostering a culture of generosity also applies deeply to for-profit companies. Generosity influences corporate culture as it does foundations, grantmaking organizations, and nonprofits that rely on charity to sustain their mission.

Is the conflict apparent? When grantmakers support specific initiatives, it becomes a communication issue to persuade supporters to align their interests with those of the grantmaker. It becomes much more difficult to convince supporters that their act of generosity truly fulfills their identity instead of serving to achieve the organization's goals.

Is it time to shift the conversation around generosity from money to trust? What if the practice of fundraising turned from "the ask" to equipping the supporter with opportunities to grow through acts of personal generosity instead of corporate and communal philanthropy?

Instead of relying upon supporters solely as a means to an outcome, what if the philanthropy sector focused on givers as active participants in creating change and on donor transfor-mation that empowers the giver to become a more generous version of themselves?

"In business, generosity flows from believing you have abundance and a desire to share, not that you have something left over to give. Philanthropy is an act of activating generosity to create impact. Charity is an action that reveals a culture of generosity."

II

Part Two

"As Jesus sat facing the temple offering box, he watched how much money people put into it. Many rich people put in large amounts. A poor widow dropped in two small coins, worth less than a cent.

He called his disciples and said to them, "I can guarantee this truth: This poor widow has given more than all the others. All of them have given what they could spare. But she, in her poverty, has given everything she had to live on."

Mark 12:41-44, GOD'S WORD Translation Bible

5

Insights from Practitioners

My perspective on "nurturing a culture of philanthropy" to "nurturing a culture of generosity" continues to evolve as my understanding of organizational culture and brand dynamics develop.

I'm trying to expand the conversation to include the people who give their time, talent, and treasure. This conversation frames a broader view on culture and its impact on your organization's brand perception.

Supporters are partners in your organization's mission, not a means to an end. To view a gift-giver in any other way is to demean philanthropy and devalue people's worth.

The concept of building a culture of philanthropy focuses on equipping the practitioner. A culture of generosity focuses on inspiring and engaging *the giver*.

What if you could do both?

Philanthropy is a practice; generosity is a virtue. When you model virtue in your practices, you begin to develop the supporter. Isn't that what fundraising and development should be about?

To explore what's possible and where there are opportunities for change, I asked fundraising experts, executive directors, and foundation CEOs three questions about philanthropy and nurturing a culture of generosity:

- As a leader, how do you advise an organization to nurture a culture of philanthropy?
- How do you recommend institutions practice a culture of generosity?
- How can an organization nurture relationships and engage people meaningfully and authentically?

In some of the responses, I've substituted *philanthropy* with *generosity* (noted in *italic*) to demonstrate that when your mindset is on the supporter and their desires, it shifts your thinking from the *function* of philanthropy to the *formation* of virtue. Hence, people listen, care, and act.

Read on to learn how Morgan Roth, Lauren Steiner, Megan Constantino, Brian Frederick, Cecilia Render, Deborah Hoover, Laura Malone, and Tom Ahern make the case for how a generosity culture can empower philanthropy and inspire supporters.

6

Build the Brand Identity and Model the Desired Behavior

Morgan Roth

* * *

Aculture of philanthropy begins – and thrives – just like any other cultural environment: when desired behaviors are modeled consistently up, down, and across an organization. Leaders of teams that have adopted sustainable philanthropy cultures empower their fundraising staff as decision-makers; however, the donor experience is owned as an organizational priority and integral to brand identity. These leaders emphasize:

- Shared responsibility for the donor experience and shared accountability for measurable and meaningful fundraising outcomes
- A consistent message that speaks directly to the core values,

23

experience, and abiding passions of those with the propensity to invest in the greater good
- A formula for ROI that is not evaluated strictly against the cost of raising a dollar, but rather against the cost of generating meaningful and sustained impact.

Although the term "culture of philanthropy" emerged in the business-speak of the sector following the publication of the Evelyn & Walter Haas Jr. Fund's *UnderDeveloped*[9] (2013) and *Fundraising Bright Spots*[10] (2016) reports, the concept of a culture that emulates the values of a community and fulfills its perceived needs has been the basis for persuading people to part with their discretionary dollars since the dawn of commerce.

The most successful "customer-first" cultures (think 'Disney') exist where earning consumers' loyalty, trust, and repeat investment is a shared responsibility from the mailroom to the board room. Mission, vision, and values are embedded in the company DNA.

A culture of *generosity* requires nonprofit communities to adopt the same core competencies and training focus that successful private-sector enterprise emphasizes for its employees: the ability to intuit and react to perceived need with empathy, the ability to articulate solutions in messaging that excites and invites, and capacity to deliver that solution consistently, effectively, and efficiently.

While one might expect that framework to prioritize mastery of direct mail, solicitation, and capital campaign strategies to ensure a vertical career trajectory, this does not.

Instead, it emphasizes the imperative of so-called "soft" strategic skills such as relationship-building, communication, organizational management, and professional judgment.

Knowledge areas, including functional aspects of managing campaigns and appeals, come after a fundraiser has demonstrated capacity to synthesize those skills in the context of good strategy and management.

Setting a course towards a culture of *generosity* begins with a collective understanding that "philanthropy" is so much more than the sum of its tactics. Annual funds, capital campaigns, and gala events are a means to an end.

Philanthropy is *what* we make of the propensity for generosity, not *how* we mine it.

The process continues with commitment from the top of the hierarchy to empower teams to work cross-functionally towards jointly owned philanthropic goals and objectives. Concurrently leaders commit to ready their fundraisers to *lead*, not merely to *participate* in sustaining a culture that prioritizes alignment and engagement with cherished stakeholders.

* * *

Morgan Roth is currently the Senior Vice President, Communication & Marketing at The ALS Association[11]. Her insights invite you to consider how identity and behavior can inspire donors when you model what generosity looks like for the everyday philanthropist.

7

Setting the Right Tone

Lauren Steiner

* * *

Nonprofit leaders absolutely set the tone in their organization and have the power to foster a culture of philanthropy. To do so, they must set their focus on two key questions:

1. Is our organization truly making the change/impact on the world it seeks to make?

Nonprofit leaders who bravely face this hard question are winning at the game of philanthropy. They are not afraid to look objectively at the programs and initiatives they are running and assess whether they are successful by this very mission-focused measure. For some, this may involve a shift in emphasis from "are we meeting our budget?" to "are we making this change we seek to make?" This requires bravery and faith, and when combined with #2 below, it can create the powerful combination of an active culture of philanthropy at work.

2. Are we consistently and openly seeking out people to join us in that effort?

Nonprofit organizations exist for the public good. As custodians of these entities, nonprofit leaders must ensure their organizations are constantly engaging people in the change/impact effort. Most people want to do good in their lives and leave a positive impact on the world. Nonprofit leaders who relentlessly seek out and engage those who want to change the world in the ways that their organization is doing so win at the game of philanthropy.

* * *

High performing nonprofit organizations with an embedded culture of *generosity* demonstrate this culture at all levels. Boards of these organizations focus on mission as much as they focus on the bottom line. They are unafraid to share the mission with their networks and others by sharing stories and the context of their own personal connection to the organization and its work. Staff leadership focuses on the mission as a lens through which all things are measured, asking: *does this further the organization's mission and its ability to make progress toward attaining it?*

For a culture of *generosity* to thrive at an organization, all staff levels understand philanthropy's value to the organization and are open and willing to do what it takes to foster this. Front line staff can play a key role in this equation as they are often the first (and sometimes the last) person to communicate with a potential donor.

One powerful way to assess the health of your culture of

generosity is to examine how a donor or a potential donor experiences your organization. From the initial contact to the last time you communicated with them... imagine what was that like from their perspective?

Many organizations who undertake this analysis find that while they are frequently communicating with their donors, this communication is heavily one-sided and not as individual as it could be.

The most important element of effective philanthropic relationships between an organization and its supporters is that it is a two-way street. Like any relationship, both parties must receive a benefit for it to work. It is vital to look at the relationship as an ongoing thing and not just a series of transactions, i.e., ask, receive a donation, send acknowledgment, repeat.

People give money to nonprofit organizations because of how it helps them define themselves – if you could hear their own inner dialogue, it would be saying things like "I am an arts supporter" or "I care about animals."

Even institutional givers like foundations give because of how the organization and its work fits into *their* priorities. Nonprofit representatives who excel in philanthropy understand this and spend just as much time talking about and listening to the donor as they do about the organization and its work.

* * *

Lauren Steiner is President of GrantsPlus, a company[12] that partners with client organizations as their trusted advisors to identify funders and recommend grant strategies.

8

Understanding Your Stakeholders

Megan Constantino

* * *

Nurturing a culture of *generosity* starts at the top of the organization and must be modeled through behavior and other support forms. Your actions always speak louder than your words, so if you want to create a movement within your organization, you must be the change you wish to see. Your people watch you and replicate what you do, whether good, bad, ugly, or indifferent. This isn't something that happens overnight, either.

To really create a culture of *generosity*, it has to come from the right place and be matched with an attitude and heart of resilience for the cause. One by one, you will enlist the troops, and eventually, the positive change becomes contagious.

Institutions practice a culture of *generosity* by starting with listening. What matters to your stakeholders? What makes them tick? What gets them out of bed in the morning to arrive at work on time and ready to serve? The key to picking a plan of action starts with understanding what inspires their teams. Then a careful and full circle analysis flows to a tactical and practical plan, including identifying the end goal and how results will be measured along the way.

Plan to recalibrate regularly as soon as you realize what works and what doesn't. This is where your greatest return on investment will occur and fulfill deep satisfaction from a positive impact.

Again, organizations can nurture relationships and engage people authentically when they begin at the organization's top. Nurturing meaningful relationships flow through every level of command within the organization. This plan should be one of accountability, transparency, flexibility, responsiveness, and most of all: values-centered.

Efforts done outside of a true relationship standpoint will be viewed as mere vanity. Today's stakeholder is armed with knowledge and holds high emotional intelligence. They will quickly recognize shallow motives.

If you aren't genuinely interested in creating a generous culture, save your energy, money, and time by not doing this at all. The exponential level of high morale that can be created in an amazing philanthropic plan can equally tank your reputation should it be for any reason other than the right.

* * *

Megan Constantino offered these insights from her experience as a former executive of a university foundation.

9

Talking the Talk

Brian Frederick

* * *

If the work fueled by philanthropy could make money, it would be part of the for-profit economy. Philanthropy exists to do the unpopular, impact the most difficult, and make possible socially beneficial purposes that are not financially feasible on their own.

I believe what drives philanthropy is essentially passion in its many forms.

- **Quiet passion** tugs as one's heartstrings until action is catalyzed.
- Philanthropy can be driven by **activist passion** that causes one to step out beyond personal comfort to advocate against injustice.
- **Empathic passion** when one can truly understand what walking in another's shoes might actually entail.

- **Blessed passion** drives one to give because of what they receive.
- **Analytic passion** is as much about one's head and one's heart.

Passion is personal and essentially hope for something better. Nurturing a culture of philanthropy is ultimately about creating a haven for sustained hope and the work needed to make that hope a reality.

The Community Foundation of Lorain County strives to be a haven of hope in Lorain County, and how we do this is probably best described in our mission, values, and beliefs.

We connect people who care with causes that matter. We gauge actions through our values; excellence – providing the best service to all, community – putting self aside for the betterment of the whole, and integrity – always doing the right thing, and through our beliefs.

We believe that integrity is our greatest asset and value trust earned with fiscal responsibility, ethical stewardship, and transparency. The impact is difficult when hope driven passion ignores research, fails to employ sound best practices, and lives only on emotion.

We believe that access to the Community Foundation should be fair, inclusive, and equitable. Philanthropy has an unfortunate aura of being a vehicle for the wealthy. Still, the Greek origin of the term philanthropy, "love of humanity," certainly places no limits on race, gender, income, sexual orientation, etc. Some of the most amazing philanthropic impact stories involve efforts that value diversity, mandate inclusiveness, and demand equity.

We believe in purposeful and collaborative community leadership. Since philanthropy is focused on the most difficult, complex, and unpopular, no one organization or effort can go alone. We need to replace the concept of competitive advantage with the idea of collaborative impact.

And finally, we believe the perpetuity of our efforts is linked to sustainable practices, and that strategy, creativity, and adaptability are keys to thriving in a constantly changing world.

This may sound like a marketing pitch, but it is critical that any organization clearly articulates who we are, what we do, and why we do what we do.

We need to *talk the talk* within the organization, so we are all pointing in the same direction and outside the organization. Our stakeholders can hold us accountable and as an invitation to potential stakeholders. Then we need to put in our earbuds, lace our cross-trainers, and use our own words to guide our collective journey forward.

* * *

Consultant **Brian Frederick** speaks from his experience as the former President & CEO of the Community Foundation of Lorain County.

10

Engaging Employees in Shared Values and Actions

Cecilia Render

* * *

I have the distinct pleasure of upholding a spirit of philanthropy initiated by the founders of Nordson Corporation, Eric and Evan Nord. I was able to step into a culture of philanthropy; the nurturing and sustaining of that culture is my pleasure and responsibility.

I feel that it is important for me to show our executives and employees how we can make a difference in the lives of those less fortunate than us in the community. I cannot say that my leadership keeps the culture going; I try to keep the community's needs at the forefront.

Our board, which is made up of corporate executives, goes on site tours to see firsthand what is going on in the community. We have had our employees take buses to see nonprofits and have had nonprofit fairs where the nonprofits come to us. If people are aware of the needs around them, they will step up to the plate. At least that is what I have seen in my fellow Nordson employees."

"At the corporate level, we donate 5% of pre-tax profit to our foundation. 5% for a corporation is above and beyond what most corporations commit to charity, and most give around 1%. Our employees already know that we as a business value philanthropy. It used to be that only the Foundation staff were involved in the grant-making process. But we decided that it is important for our employees to feel that they are a part of our value system, so we now have employees who volunteer their time to review grants, go on site visits and make recommendations to the board on our giving.

These Community Affairs Committees (CAC) give our employees ownership and allow them to see firsthand the local communities' needs and how we can help as a corporation. We also try to support the charitable interests of our employees. We do that by supporting their volunteerism.

If an employee has a nonprofit where they like to volunteer their time, we will grant that organization a grant once the employee has donated 40 hours within a year. There are different names for it, but our program is called Dollars for Doers. We also have a matching gift program that doubles the amount that an employee donates up to $10,000 per year."

It is important to get to know the people in any organization that you are supporting through philanthropy. Grant request time is not the only time that the two should get together. I do not think it is the role of philanthropy to tell nonprofits what to do. I think that we should be partners in a process. I think that if we are all authentic in those partnerships that relationships and engagement will grow naturally.

It is not possible as a funder to support every organization that requests money. But it is possible to be a resource to all organizations. I hope at the end of the day that anyone that we were not able to financially support, for whatever reason, still walks away with something positive, whether that be an idea, a reference, a volunteer, or a board member.

* * *

Cecilia Render, the Nordson Corporation Foundation[13] Executive Director, speaks from decades of experience guiding the corporate philanthropy office's generous intent.

11

Participate with the Causes You Support

Deborah Hoover

* * *

Burton D. Morgan Foundation's philanthropy culture is deeply rooted in our founder's charitable vision, who explicitly connected his goals for the foundation of his career as a serial entrepreneur. While he reveled in the excitement and resources his ventures generated, he also recognized his responsibility to give back to the community that fostered his success. In my role as leader of the foundation, it is fundamental that I reflect on our donor's generosity and donor intent as I help to guide our strategic direction and optimize Mr. Morgan's wishes in support of entrepreneurship in Northeast Ohio.

It is an important charge and one that I take very seriously. I encourage our team to keep Mr. Morgan's magnanimous spirit as a beacon for our work. Even though the foundation is now almost fifty years old, we continue to embrace his wisdom and adapt his ideas to the challenges confronting our region today.

To this end, we maintain Mr. Morgan's image and words as an integral part of our daily work and decision making.

Morgan Foundation believes that the practice of philanthropy requires adherence to the highest standards of ethical conduct, judicious use of foundation assets, and energetic pursuit of research and information to inform our decisions.

Our foundation strives to serve as a role model for others, always stretching the boundaries and ensuring that the lessons derived from our grantmaking are reinvested in our own work and shared with our colleagues. We are active participants in the professional organizations that support philanthropy and greatly value the bonds we forge through these learning communities and shared experiences.

While the financial resources Mr. Morgan dedicated to the foundation are our primary asset, these resources are properly deployed, yield a host of other resources in the form of knowledge, experience, networks, and collaborations. These additional capabilities form the basis of the close relationships we maintain with our grantees—bonds carefully crafted to achieve common goals.

We nurture these relationships through open communication, the investment of time and thought, and the back and forth exchange of information as we explore new frontiers together. In our view, this is ideal philanthropic practice and helps us to remain true to the faith Mr. Morgan placed in us as we carry on his legacy and ensure that his vision lives on. It is indeed an enormous responsibility and one that our foundation trustees and staff do not take lightly.

* * *

Deborah Hoover is President & CEO of The Burton D. Morgan Foundation[14], a private foundation that provides grants to nonprofit organizations working in entrepreneurship and entrepreneurship education at the youth, collegiate, and adult levels.

12

Share Your Donor's Stories

Laura Malone

* * *

This may sound cliché, but one of the first things I truly believe is that a leader needs to live a culture of *generosity* before they can nurture it in others. The work I did at American Endowment Foundation is a passion, and I like to think that it resonated in a noticeable way to others. I love to share stories of donors and the other advisors we collaborate with through our program.

I believe this helps me to be able to nurture an understanding among my coworkers and other collaborators about the importance of our role in philanthropy. As a leader, I feel it is very important to "walk the talk" and do not feel comfortable asking others to embrace something I have not.

The first thing American Endowment Foundation does as an institution is to make a conscious effort to hire people whose personalities, attitudes, values, and competencies exemplify the culture we are trying to create and maintain.

While skill sets are important, nothing is more important to us than ensuring our teams have aligned energy. I also believe our focus on customer service is extremely important in this case.

As a national Donor Advised Fund (DAF) program, our donors are our partners, and the best way we can help them is to make their philanthropy as easy as possible. We would be nothing without our donors, and I think we remain fully cognizant of that every day in everything we do. I think this has gone a long way in our donor retention over the years. It is best exemplified when donors are presented with opportunities to choose another DAF solution but choose to remain with us because they are delighted with how we nurture our relationship.

Our work as a charity that provides donor-advised funds does not always present us with the same challenges other nonprofits may face. In speaking with other organizations, I will say there seems to be a challenge in balancing focus on both the organization's impact on society and its operational efficiency. From "the outside looking in," it appears that organizations often sometimes lose sight of the former while focusing on the latter.

One of the first things that can be done is really embracing from the board to the staff that the charitable work any organization does rely first and foremost on relationships – not just with who they serve, but with who they partner with and those that support the organization. To really be meaningful and authentic, strong relationships need time to nurture and grow. They will not happen overnight.

This may mean more of a focus on long-term goals rather than short-term results. Leadership has to give their staff time to explore, create, and deepen these relationships, so the culture of philanthropy can be what it is meant to be – transformational.

* * *

Currently a development officer in a community foundation, **Laura Malone** worked with generous people every day as the Director of Corporate/Complex Giving of the American Endowment Foundation (AEF)[15], an independent donor-advised fund program.

13

Don't Ignore People Who Support You

Tom Ahern

* * *

You start where you have the most control: at all the touchpoints you have with your donors.

These would include your charity's website (home page and giving page), emailed appeals and newsletters, direct mail appeals, new-donor welcome packs, print newsletters, thank you notes, and annual reports.

The most common messaging problem I've seen is this: they don't know that your mission needs donors. This problem arises for a couple of reasons.

First, charities go on in a naively egocentric way about how great their work is, assuming this will impress. That approach is fine when you're speaking to foundations. But it's exactly the wrong approach when raising money from individuals. Most charities in my observation (and I see hundreds of examples a year) ignore donors' importance. Their communications are "donor optional," not "donor-centered." Often, they ignore the donor's emotional needs altogether. Donors exist merely as life-support systems for a wallet. They have no other apparent value.

Second, charities send subconscious cues that somebody else's money will foot the bill. The classic meme is the "big check photo." In a donor newsletter, what that particular photo says at a hundred miles an hour is: "We don't need your money. We already have a bunch."

Third, charities do not offer donors something important to do.

My definition of a culture of philanthropy is pragmatic. It means each staff member and volunteer (and those served, for that matter) understands that philanthropy is vital to the mission.

I had the disturbing experience of working with a well-regarded, NYC-based advocacy charity that's been fighting the good fight for 50 years. I asked the executive director, "What do the board and staff think of fundraising?" He said with satisfaction in his voice, "We think of it as a necessary evil."

This, in my view, fully explained why this NYC nonprofit had assembled about 2,500 donors after 50 years ... while a similar advocacy group that had started about the same time now had 3 million donors.

* * *

Tom Ahern is an author and the founder of Ahern Communications[16], a consultancy focusing on donor communications.

III

Part Three

Your brand's role is to guide the giver and help them direct their generosity toward their goals.

That's what philanthropy is all about: the people who care.

14

Practical Guidance for Leaders

C ulture is complex, yet there are fundamental and core beliefs and resolute values within every organization. Where generosity and the practice of generosity are deeply held beliefs, your organization will instinctively demonstrate its relevance through the way it treats people and nurtures relationships.

In this way, people will understand the organization practices a culture of generosity that drives their philanthropic intent.

Let's rephrase that for supporters: In the most effective organizations, *a culture of generosity understands donor motivations and helps them achieve their goals.*

Fostering a culture of generosity is about developing a culture where you help people outside your organization understand their identity as generous people. Your organization becomes a means for them to express that generosity.

In order to achieve this type of brand culture, there are two challenges[17] that each organization must overcome.

The first challenge in developing generosity culture is to create alignment between the organization's brand promise (*what it believes and how it expresses those beliefs*) and the supporter's values (*what they believe about the organization and how they expect you to express those beliefs*).

The second challenge in developing generosity culture is to develop clear and aligned communications that consistently align with the brand's character and personality.

In this section, look for practical advice and practices that empower you to put what you learned in Part Two into practice.

15

Be a Brand People Love

Organizations often overlook a brand's relational aspects with all the effort spent on management techniques and acquisition strategies.

Why are some brands celebrated by legions of raving fans?

How does it make you feel when you compare your brand to theirs?

Here are six ways to be (or become) a brand people love:

1. First —**don't compare** unless the other brand or organization is a direct competitor.
2. **If you must compare, do it to learn**. Figure out how they are making their customers or supporters the hero and how they make them feel.
3. **Build your foundation from the ground up:** Clarify your brand truth and mission, create a clear message[18] and story that connects with customers, and then build a marketing plan to share your voice, message, and impact with the world.

According to a report from Forrester, "Studies show consumers value human-like communication from brands." According to the report, 60% of brand experiences result in human-like connections. That's important, considering that 57% of consumers say that human communication would increase their brand loyalty, and 58% say human communication would increase their likelihood of spending money with a given brand.[19]

If a trusted source doesn't refer a prospective supporter,[20] it's up to you to inform, inspire, and engage them:

1. **Ask for permission.** Give prospects a simple first step to move them from observers to participants. Offer them something that will add value to their lives in exchange for permission to market to them.
2. **Allow people to engage** in a meaningful way. Now that they're paying attention ask for their feedback or feedback on what's important to them. Offer them an opportunity to do something that will help them grow.
3. **Prepare to steward the relationship**. As people become givers, offer them opportunities, experiences, and services that make them feel good and transform them in ways that matter to them. These people become the brand ambassadors representing your cause wherever they go because your brand's values and ideals have become part of the individual's story.

When you focus on value to givers (and less on what is important for your organization), your brand is more likely to see increased engagement and growth.

That's what building a brand people love is all about.

16

Speak with One Brand Voice

Every brand ambassador needs to speak with one voice when they represent the organization, and everyone has the potential to be a brand ambassador.

The president, executive director, or CEO of any business or nonprofit is tasked with being a brand ambassador. Everyone associated with the cause and the organization has the *potential* to be a brand ambassador.

Message, Story, and Authenticity

- "Keep your story straight."
- "Stay on message."
- "These are the talking points."

Each of these phrases is more about presentation than about practice. Words can be rehearsed, conversations can be practiced, and speakers can be prepped for what they will say. What truly resonates with an audience is authenticity – when what is said and how it is delivered is natural, confident, sincere, and uplifting.

The core messages aren't stories. The core messages are the foundation upon which stories are created, and they serve as the filter for what stories support the organization's purpose. The core messages are built upon facts and information, formed from the purpose for which the organization exists, and are the elements of truth that will inform your audience.

Stories are what inspire your audience. Good storytelling can come from various sources – the design and communication team, testimonials from your audience, and everyday experience in delivering programs and services. Good stories have the potential to touch the heart and motivate listeners to action.

Stories can be truthful, or stories can be made up. We've all read fiction, heard fairy tales, and certainly have seen a nonprofit represents itself through fictionalized stories. We've heard speakers embellish the message's truth with a story we later find out was untrue.

Simply reciting core messaging and telling stories does not convey authenticity. As an ambassador and advocate, you should reach a point where you act and behave, and how you speak and listen flows from within – because you believe it and are living it. You either believe in what you're doing, or you don't.

You can't fake authenticity.

Your audience may not notice the lack of authenticity initially, but there will be clues over time. In announcements made on the web site, in the volunteer experience, you may see hints that something has changed in marketing and promotional materials, but you can't quite put your finger on it.

This is your organization's voice – the words were spoken, messages that are shared, and touchpoints that appeal to our ears, eyes, and minds – and must be as carefully guarded as spoken words.

How many times have you thought, *"I wish I would not have said that,"* after the fact?

The truth of authenticity is always revealed in the spoken expression of a brand ambassador. The written word gives the author the luxury of review. Speaking engagements must be designed and planned and allow minimal opportunities for off-the-cuff remarks.

Those in positions of authority and leadership have a responsibility to their cause and their constituents. Our actions show the way we think; our words express what is in our hearts. Action reveals thoughts and words reflect the heart – what we believe and what motivates us. Authenticity is eventually revealed through words and actions.

The Heart and Mind of a Brand Ambassador

You believe that your cause has the power to change the world. You believe that the core message points are true and speak them from the heart because your mind has acknowledged that they are true.

You've become a brand ambassador – living the cause with the conviction of character – when your words flow from believing in the purpose and values that define your organization.

You've moved from being a follower to a believer that will live and give sacrificially.

This Is Who We Are

We are all brand ambassadors. As a brand ambassador, you can role-play, or you can live with purpose.

If you are involved with a nonprofit representing a cause that matters, you are a brand ambassador.

If you tell friends about your favorite products and services, you're a brand ambassador.

When you are a raving fan or brand ambassador, you represent the cause and brand. You'll build trust and credibility for yourself and the brand when you know your role and authentic in your storytelling.

The outcomes from following a set of guiding principles that enable you to speak with one voice – supporting your purpose, character, and culture – create design continuity and culture of authenticity, accountability, transparency, and trust.

17

Put Gratitude First

A culture of generosity begins with gratitude.

Being grateful is a principle that acknowledges to your supporters that their gifts are meaningful. Gratefulness recognizes that the gift is important and will make a difference. Being grateful is *understanding how the giver feels about giving and what their gift means to them*, not about the gift itself. Gratefulness is a cultural practice.

Successful organizations make this one of their guiding principles:

We will express our gratitude to our supporters, remembering that their gifts are meaningful and their generosity makes a difference.

Regardless of the type, every donation must be acknowledged. Here's how you can make an immediate difference that your supporters will notice:

- Say *Thank You*—first, fast, and foremost for every gift, no matter its size.

- Think acknowledgment first, and if appropriate, donor recognition second. An individual may forget what you do or say in response to their gift, but they won't forget how you made them feel.
- Does every gift receive a thank you letter or note? Does every gift receive the same letter? If so, at what level does the executive director or an advancement officer write a brief personal note to acknowledge the donor's gift? At what level do they receive a personal phone call?
- Do you have a threshold for which acknowledgments are given special attention? Are $5,000 gifts acknowledged differently than a $50 gift?
- Do you consider what kind of sacrifice their gift means to the giver?
- Touch your supporter's heart. Their decision to give was made with their mind, but their gift is from the heart. Think of your donor and how your gift acknowledgment (or lack of) will make them feel. Your response could determine the potential for future giving—possibly in greater ways—or cause the supporter to consider how their gift could create an impact elsewhere.
- For special campaigns (such as capital or major gift campaigns), do you acknowledge gifts differently than you do for general operating support?

18

Master the Art of Donor Storytelling

Does the thought of capturing your supporter's stories feel overwhelming?

As a leader, we know you're already a great listener. But if you are managing people's financial gifts without also stewarding their story, your organization is missing out on a critical inspirational asset that will help you multiply a gift-givers' generosity. When you multiply generosity through the power of stories, your organization grows.

Here's some good news! You can learn to steward stories of generosity.

To do that, you need to become a trusted story gatherer to become a confident storyteller.

Because many organizations (especially community foundations) only capture a portion of the gift a supporter is willing to share with them, your organization's impact doesn't grow as quickly as it could because leaders are missing out on the opportunity to multiply the financial gifts they receive.

Your brand's role is to be a guide who comes alongside

the giver (the real hero in your story) to help them direct
their generosity toward their goals.

Story gathering focuses on the giver and their reasons for generosity. While it may be tempting to position your organization as the hero, its role is a guide and partner who comes alongside the supporter (the real hero in your story) to help them direct their generosity.

When you are story gathering, listen for opportunities that allow you to share why the supporter choose your organization as the preferred recipient of their gift. Listen inquisitively for shared values that drew them to your organization.

Start a conversation with your supporters with these questions:

- Is there a particular cause you care about deeply?
- What inspires you to make the community a better place?
- What do the people you want to help need?
- Why do you want to be generous?
- What do you care about in our community?
- What are some of your giving goals this year and for your lifetime?
- How does giving make you feel?
- Where do you think your gift can make the most significant difference?
- Whose life will be changed because of your gift?
- What prompted you to take the next step and make a generous donation?
- How will the people you helped experience better lives because of your gift?

People love to talk about their lives, their experiences, and the things they love. The giver sitting in front of you isn't just a donor — it's a person with dreams, goals, and passion for the things that matter to them.

When you share people's joy, they understand you care about them. When they understand your care, they want you to participate in *their* generosity.

> *Start with empathy to understand what is important to*
> *the people who give and how you can help them become*
> *the generous giver they dream of being.*
> Brian Sooy

Listen carefully, and people will tell you everything to need to hear so you can take what they share and weave a story worth telling.

19

Twelve Principles to Nurture a Culture of Generosity

Many leaders struggle to create a brand that aligns purpose, character, communication, and voice so their culture and organization flourish.

The Brand Clarity Credo empowers leaders with 12 essential principles to grow their brand and nurture generous culture.

Implementing these will require the resolve and courage to reinvent your brand, and the results will be worth all the effort.

1. **Be Strategic.** We will create and follow a plan that aligns our character, culture, and voice with our mission, vision, and values.
2. **Be Focused.** We will eliminate distractions to pursue the opportunities that enable us to fulfill our mission and achieve our vision.
3. **Be Meaningful.** We will stay true to the values and actions that inspire people to support our vision and the difference we make.
4. **Be Insightful.** We will seek clarity and a greater under-

standing of the results of our mission, vision, and impact.

5. **Be Inspiring**. We will speak to the mind and appeal to the heart with stories that inspire people to listen, care, and act.

6. **Be Engaging.** We will be curious, listening closely to discover, hear, and understand what people value and expect of us.

7. **Be Social.** We will be ambassadors, recognizing that every interaction is an opportunity to build and strengthen relationships.

8. **Be Grateful.** We will acknowledge the people who share our values, believe in our vision, and help us make a difference.

9. **Be Trustworthy**. We will be accountable and transparent, speaking, and acting true to our purpose, character, culture, and voice.

10. **Be Positive**. We will choose our words wisely because they inspire people to trust, follow, take action, and make a difference.

11. **Be Powerful**. We will act boldly and speak confidently because our purpose and vision has the power to change people's lives.

12. **Be Courageous.** We will be fearless and resilient, overcoming every challenge as we lead the movement to achieve our vision.

When you join the Brand Clarity movement, you receive a free poster and weekly insights featuring twelve principles that will help you define your purpose, build your brand, deepen relationships, and develop leadership for a high-performance culture.

Join the Brand Clarity movement today and get the inspiration and practical guidance to help you achieve greater clarity for your brand, business, and culture.

Download a complimentary poster[21] to share these principles with your team.

20

What's Next for Your Brand?

I f you don't put what you learned into action, it's like looking in a mirror and forgetting what you look like once you walk away.

- Measure how supporters and stakeholders perceive your organization's brand personality with a Brand Reflections assessment[22] from Aespire.
- Work with Aespire[23] to clarify your strategy[24] and align your communications, so supporters are the hero in your story.

Read the Aespire Blogs

- Read the Aespire Brand Clarity Blog[25] for insights on building a relationship brand.
- Read the My Lasting Legacy blog[26] to master the art of engaging generous people.

Download an Aespire Branding Guide

Read Amazon's Top-Rated Nonprofit Branding Book

Inspire generosity through the principles from "Raise Your Voice: A Cause Manifesto,"[27] the top-rated book that helps boards and leaders build meaningful mission-driven brands.

Download a sample chapter, "Be Grateful,"[28] to learn why reviewers say,

> *"Raise Your Voice is a terrific book for any organization that wants to gain clarity with their communications to achieve greater impact. It offers both inspiring and practical advice and lots of examples to help nonprofits be courageous, engaging, focused, and strategic. I highly recommend it!" – Kristen Putnam Walkerly, Putnam Consulting*

Master the Art of Visual Storytelling

When you tell a story with infographics, typography, and design, you can turn numbers and research data into a visual narrative that helps the viewer see with their mind what they feel with their heart.

Infographics can help you capture the relevance, value, and uniqueness of your company or cause, and make a case for why people should buy, donate, advocate, and take action.

- Download the Aespire *Visual Storytelling Guide*[29] to learn how you can connect with people's hearts and minds and create a greater impact!

Master the Art of Donor Storytelling

**Does the thought of capturing your donor's stories feel over-
whelming?** *It doesn't have to be.* You can learn to steward stories
of generosity. To do that, you need to become a trusted story
gatherer to become a confident storyteller.

Because many foundations only capture half of the gift a donor
is willing to share with them, the foundation's assets don't grow
as quickly as they could because leaders are missing out on the
opportunity to multiply the financial gifts they receive.

- Download Aespire's **Art of Donor Storytelling Guide**[30] and
  learn the art of gathering and sharing stories that unlock
  the power of legacy giving.

Notes

PREFACE

1   https://www.mylastinglegacy.org/blog/5-ways-to-honor-small-gifts

IS PHILANTHROPY A PRACTICE OR A VIRTUE?

2   A framework for understanding what a culture of philanthropy might look
    like, and provides suggestions on how to know if you have one.
    https://www.haasjr.org/resources/beyond-fundraising

3   From "Strategic Fund Development: Building Profitable Relationships That
    Last," available at https://amzn.to/3oQKCFQ

GENEROSITY IS A BRANDING CHALLENGE

4   The Charities Aid Foundation explores questions defining charitable behav-
    ior across the world https://www.cafamerica.org/world-giving-index/

5   https://nccs.urban.org/project/national-taxonomy-exempt-entities-ntee-
    codes
    The National Taxonomy of Exempt Entities (NTEE) system is used by
    the IRS and NCCS to classify nonprofit organizations. It is also used by the
    Foundation Center to classify both grants and grant recipients (typically
    nonprofits or governments).

6   "Raise Your Voice: A Cause Manifesto," Brian Sooy, 2014. Buy it at
    go.aespire.com/RYV

7   Marketing to Mindstates: The Practical Guide to Applying Behavior Design
    to Research and Marketing, Will Leach, 2018.

8   Author and researcher Will Leach identify the nine core motivations:
    achievement, autonomy, belonging, competence, empowerment, engage-
    ment, esteem, nurturance, and security. *Marketing to Mindstates*, page 114

BUILD THE BRAND IDENTITY AND MODEL THE DESIRED BEHAVIOR

9   A joint project of CompassPoint and the Evelyn and Walter Haas, Jr. Fund,
    this study found high levels of turnover and lengthy vacancies in de-

velopment director positions throughout the sector, as well as deeper organizational issues. https://www.haasjr.org/resources/underdeveloped

10 Fundraising Bright Spots explores how a select group of social change organizations are achieving breakthrough results in individual giving. https://www.haasjr.org/resources/fundraising-bright-spots

11 https://www.als.org

SETTING THE RIGHT TONE

12 https://grantsplus.com

ENGAGING EMPLOYEES IN SHARED VALUES AND ACTIONS

13 https://www.nordson.com/en/our-company/community/leaders-in-nordson-philanthropy

PARTICIPATE WITH THE CAUSES YOU SUPPORT

14 https://www.bdmorganfdn.org

SHARE YOUR DONOR'S STORIES

15 https://www.aefonline.org

DON'T IGNORE PEOPLE WHO SUPPORT YOU

16 https://www.aherncomm.com

PRACTICAL GUIDANCE FOR LEADERS

17 Read more about these branding and culture challenges at https://www.my-lastinglegacy.org/blog/two-challenges-of-nonprofit-communications

BE A BRAND PEOPLE LOVE

18 https://www.aespire.com/expertise/storybrand-marketing

19 https://www.braze.com/resources/library/report/what-makes-a-brand-human

20 https://www.aespire.com/blog/why-trust-is-important-to-your-brand-and-business

TWELVE PRINCIPLES TO NURTURE A CULTURE OF GENEROSITY

21 https://www.aespire.com/resources/brand-clarity-principles

WHAT'S NEXT FOR YOUR BRAND?

22 https://www.aespire.com/grow/clear-messaging

23 https://www.aespire.com

24 https://www.aespire.com/grow/begin-with-strategy

25 https://www.aespire.com/blog

26 https://www.mylastinglegacy.org/blog

27 https://www.aespire.com/resources/raise-your-voice-book

28 http://dl.bookfunnel.com/1dwq8x2f1n

29 https://www.aespire.com/resources/visual-brand-storytelling-guide

30 https://www.mylastinglegacy.org/art-of-storytelling

About the Author

Brian Sooy is the president of Aespire (Aespire.com), the branding and marketing agency that helps people build relationship brands. As a StoryBrand Certified Guide, Brian helps business owners and entrepreneurs gain confidence that their marketing investment creates ROI and helps them grow their business.

Brian is recognized as one of Relevance.com's *Top 100 Marketing Influencers to Follow* and is the author of several books, including *Raise Your Voice: A Cause Manifesto*, the top-rated guide for mission-driven leaders.

You can connect with me on:

- https://www.aespire.com
- https://twitter.com/briansooy
- https://www.mylastinglegacy.org
- https://www.linkedin.com/in/briansooy
- https://www.relevance.com/the-top-100-marketing-influencers-to-follow-in-2020
- https://www.clarifyyourmessage.com/Brian-Sooy

Subscribe to my newsletter:

✉ https://www.aespire.com/resources/brand-clarity-principles

Also by Brian G. Sooy

Raise Your Voice: A Cause Manifesto
https://go.aespire.com/RYVCM
Filled with insights into how strategic communications attract, engage, and retain supporters, "Raise Your Voice" is a guidebook that enables your cause to fulfill its promise and invite your donors to be part of the difference you make in people's lives.

This guidebook is full of practical insight for helping mission-driven organizations that struggle with branding and communications build deeper relationships and tell stories that resonate with people so they listen, care, act, and donate.